THE
MELBOURNE TRAM

RANDALL WILSON   DALE

UNSW PRESS

A UNSW Press book

Published by
University of New South Wales Press Ltd
University of New South Wales
Sydney NSW 2052
AUSTRALIA
www.unswpress.com.au

© Randall Wilson and Dale Budd 2003, 2008
First published 2003
Reprinted with updates 2005
Second edition 2008

National Library of Australia
Cataloguing-in-Publication entry

Wilson, Randall, 1951– .
  The Melbourne tram book.
  ISBN 978 1 921410 49 9.
  1. Trams – Victoria – Melbourne.
  2. Tramways – Victoria – Melbourne.
  I. Budd, Dale. II. Title.
  388.46099451

Design Dana Lundmark
Printer Everbest, China

ACKNOWLEDGMENTS

The authors gratefully acknowledge the assistance of the many individuals and organisations who, by making available photographs
and paintings, made this book possible. Much
of its content is drawn from *Melbourne's
Marvellous Trams*, by the same authors,
published by UNSW Press in 1998.
    The authors also thank David Jones and
Alan Pritchard for their expert cartography
and drawings of trams; ALSTOM Australia
(now United Group) and Siemens Australia
for permission to reproduce tram drawings;
and the Victorian Department of Infrastructure
for permission to reproduce material on the
City Circle tram service and the Hawthorn
Depot Museum.

Front cover photographs by the authors,
except • *bottom left* Stuart McEvoy, Leader
Community Newspapers • *bottom right*
Public Records Office of Victoria • *Back
cover photograph* William F Scott • *Inside
cover photographs* by the authors •
Previous page W series tram in Bourke
Street at dusk *WJ Niven* • For other picture
credits please see page 80.

FURTHER READING

For information on Melbourne's cable trams
and the routes on which they ran:

Jack Cranston, *The Melbourne Cable Trams
1885 to 1940*, Craftsman Publishing,
Melbourne, 1988.

John D Keating, *Mind the Curve! A History
of the Cable Trams*, Transit Australia
Publishing, Sydney, 1996.

For information on Melbourne's electric
trams from 1889 to the present:

Dale Budd and Randall Wilson,
Melbourne's Marvellous Trams,
UNSW Press, Sydney, 1998.

Norman Cross, Dale Budd and
Randall Wilson, *Destination City*,
Transit Australia Publishing, Sydney, 1993.

For information on Melbourne's tramway
system:

David R Keenan, *Melbourne Tramways*,
Transit Press, Sydney, 1985.

CONTENTS

MELBOURNE AND ITS TRAMS

Many cities have tram systems, but between Melbourne and its trams there is a special relationship.

Melbourne is alone among Australian cities in retaining a large tram network. When other Australian cities discarded their trams in the mid-20th century, Melbourne had the foresight to buck the trend. More recently, the fleet of trams has been renewed and the system extended.

Perhaps it was this determination to stick with trams, against the fashion of the time, that led to the affection many Melburnians have for them. From time to time, issues affecting the trams have stirred strong public interest: ticketing, crewing and the retention of older trams have been major topics of public debate. Trams have featured in Moomba parades and have appeared in films and television series. They have been the subject of works of art and some have even become works of art themselves.

Not everyone has warm feelings for the trams. Motorists may view them with impatience. For those who use them, however, they are accessible and reliable. They provide more than a vital public transport service: they are a symbol of the city. Without the trams, Melbourne's streets would seem strangely empty.

This book shows something of the links that have existed for more than a century between Melbourne, its people and its trams. We hope you enjoy our coverage of trams and people in one of the world's most liveable cities.

Randall Wilson   Dale Budd

ERA OF THE CABLE TRAMS

Melbourne's first cable tram ran almost continuously for 55 years until 1940. Faithfully restored by the tramways staff of the Preston Workshops, it is now on display at the Science-works science museum in the inner south-western suburb of Spotswood.

Like San Francisco and Chicago, Melbourne was one of the great, fast-growing cities of the late 19th century. Yet little remains today of Melbourne's cable tram network, which exceeded San Francisco's in size and was one of the most efficient and technically advanced in the world.

Designed and built essentially as a single entity between 1885 and 1891, Melbourne's cable tram system epitomised sophistication and excellence in city transport at the time of its construction. On completion the system comprised nearly 75 kilometres of double track serving 17 routes.

For most of its life the system was operated by the Melbourne Tramway and Omnibus Company, until it passed into government ownership in 1916. At that time the company was operating 480 grip cars (known as 'dummies'), 460 standard four-wheel trailer cars and 56 larger bogie trailers.

From the early 1920s, it became clear that the cable system could not meet the transport requirements of the steadily expanding city. Sixteen years after closure of the city's first cable line, Melbourne's last cable tram ran on 26 October 1940, decades before the historical significance of the system would have been appreciated by governments or many of the city's citizens.

Collins Street Melbourne Victoria.

▷ Well-dressed women have a panoramic view from the front of a grip car as they travel down fashionable Collins Street past the Town Hall.

▷ Swanston Street and St Kilda Road were the busiest of Melbourne's cable tram lines, serving the south-eastern suburbs of Toorak, Windsor and Prahran. Having negotiated its way through a multitude of delivery wagons and carts in the city's commercial heart, a lightly loaded cable tram heads towards Princes Bridge and the system's most southerly destination of Brighton Road.

▷ 'A glimpse of Collins Street ...' Cable trams bound for Port Melbourne and North Fitzroy pass near the site of today's city square.

◁ In the years when horse-drawn vehicles were synonymous with road transport, the cable tram symbolised cleanliness and efficiency. In this Edwardian scene in Collins Street, affluent city shoppers and other pedestrians wait for a cable tram to pass en route to middle-class North Fitzroy.

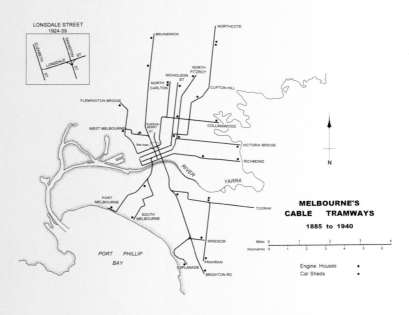

See inset

LONSDALE STREET
1924-39

MELBOURNE'S
CABLE TRAMWAYS
1885 to 1940

Engine Houses
Car Sheds

PORT PHILLIP BAY

△ Melbourne's first cable tram route, built in 1885, connected the city with the inner working-class suburb of Richmond, some six kilometres east of the city. With Hosie's Hotel on its left, a Richmond-bound tram approaches Elizabeth Street before ascending the grade to the busy junction with Swanston Street.

▽ Successive decades of prosperity in the latter half of the 19th century, culminating in the speculative extravagance of 'Marvellous Melbourne' in the 1880s, gave the city a heritage of fine public buildings. In this scene dating from the 1890s, an in-bound cable tram glides past the colony's Treasury towards the intersection of Spring and Collins streets.

▽ The signing of the Armistice on 11 November 1918 was celebrated throughout the British Empire by the decoration of buildings and public places. Public transport had some special roles during the war, being used first to promote recruitment and later to help celebrate the eventual victory.

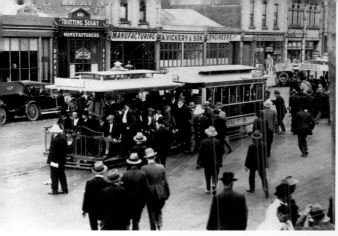

◁ For over 100 years, trams have played their part in moving people to and from sporting events ranging from football and cricket to the Olympic Games and Grand Prix motor racing. In the 1920s, trams in Bridge Road collect punters returning from the Richmond Pony Racecourse.

▽◁ Melbourne's cable trams comprised two units: a grip car (or dummy), which towed a saloon car (right). The order of the two vehicles had to be reversed at the terminus of each route, often with the assistance of passengers. This mid-1920s scene shows a reversing movement underway in Domain Road near St Kilda Road.

◁ A cable tram gripman pauses for a photograph during shunting movements at the northern terminus of Nicholson Street, North Fitzroy.

◁ The first trams in the Melbourne suburbs of Coburg, Hawthorn, Kew, Caulfield and Beaumaris were drawn by horses. Most of these lines were later absorbed into the electric tram network. In a scene probably typical of the early 20th century, horses prepare to pull an overloaded car towards the terminus of the Beaumaris horse tramway.

Melbourne's first electric tram ran in 1889, on a pioneering line from Box Hill to Doncaster. This short-lived operation ceased in 1896, and it was another 10 years before electric traction returned, in the form of the much more substantial service operated by the Victorian Railways from St Kilda to Brighton Beach. In the same year, privately owned lines opened from Flemington Bridge to Essendon and the Maribyrnong River. These were both feeder services, linking respectively with steam trains at St Kilda, and cable trams at Flemington Bridge. Over the next decade, other electric lines were built as feeders to the cable network, operated by trusts formed by local councils.

THE EARLY ELECTRIC YEARS

A program of reform saw the whole network, cable and electric, brought under unified control between 1916 and 1922 with the exception of the Victorian Railways lines, which by then consisted of two routes: from St Kilda to Brighton Beach and from Sandringham to Black Rock.

The newly formed Melbourne and Metropolitan Tramways Board launched a program of conversion of the cable system to electric traction, and construction of new electric lines. This program was not effectively completed until 1956, which was also the year in which the last of the famous W series trams was placed in service.

▽ The designers of Melbourne's first electric tram must have had optimistic views about the city's climate — or about the willingness of travellers to brave the elements. This is 14 October 1889, opening day of Melbourne's, and Australia's, first electric tramway, from Box Hill to Doncaster. This tram and one other operated for some seven years on this pioneering line, which ran through open countryside. Tram design was to evolve rapidly over this period, providing much greater comfort for passengers, and greater speed and reliability.

△ Travellers from the new garden suburbs established from the early 20th century had to change from electric trams to cable trams to reach the city. At Flemington Bridge, an electric tram from Essendon (left) has just arrived, while a cable tram (centre) waits to depart for the city. An early double-deck bus and horse-drawn wagon complete this scene from around 1910.

△ Trams were elaborately decorated for special occasions, such as the openings of new lines, anniversaries or other patriotic events. This tram is about to leave Malvern Depot, decorated for the coronation of King George V in 1911.

◁ Opening day for the Prahran and Malvern Tramway Trust's line to Elsternwick: 13 November 1913. There is an air of excitement as a procession of trams makes its way along Glen Huntly Road.

▽ In the days before road transport was able to carry substantial loads, specially converted trams performed the task of moving freight between workshops and depots. Freight Car No 2A has since been restored to a 'toast-rack' passenger tram – see page 39 (bottom).

△ The usefulness of trams for advertising was recognised almost from the beginning. This open-sided tram, normally used for cleaning the track and other utilitarian duties, was decked out during the First World War to promote recruiting.

▽ Early days on the line to Ascot Vale: a North Melbourne Electric Tramways and Lighting Company tram is delayed in Racecourse Road, Newmarket, by a flock of sheep on their way to the saleyards in the 1920s. Redevelopment of the saleyards from the late 1980s transformed Newmarket into a pleasant residential suburb.

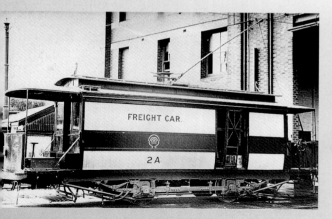

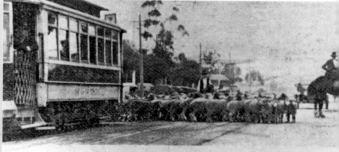

WHERE CITY AND COUNTRY MEET.—Sheep on the road to the N market yards held up traffic yesterday. Their drovers did not hold a stop- meeting, as they had threatened to do.

△ Down through the years, the completion of new tramways has often been celebrated by formal ceremonies and an element of fanfare. On 1 April 1920, officials of the Melbourne and Metropolitan Tramways Board join with locals for the departure of the first tram to East Preston.

◁ With growth in the number of motor vehicles, parking in Collins Street seems to have been a problem as early as the 1920s. While a number of historic buildings in this section of Collins Street were demolished in the postwar period, many others remain, thus preserving the 19th-century character of this part of the city.

▽ Melbourne's commercial heart in the early 1930s was relatively confined by 21st-century standards, so that its tall buildings were easily captured in this classic postcard scene. In the foreground, electric trams introduced in St Kilda Road in 1926 pass the site of today's Melbourne Concert Hall.

CITY
AND
SUBURBS

Melbourne's distinctive grid-like pattern of wide streets interspersed with tree-lined boulevards owes much to the vision of influential figures such as its first lieutenant governor, Charles La Trobe, who laid out the city's parks and gardens, and its first surveyor general, Robert Hoddle, who planned the city's major thoroughfares.

Today, trams run over nearly 250 kilometres of route, extending more than 20 kilometres from the city centre.

▽ The Yarra River, once one of Melbourne's less attractive waterways, has returned to prominence in recent years with the development of major office, retail and hotel accommodation at Southbank.

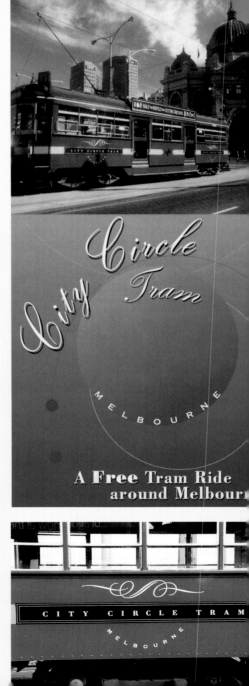

City Circle Tram
MELBOURNE

A Free Tram Ride around Melbourne

CITY CIRCLE TRAM
MELBOURNE

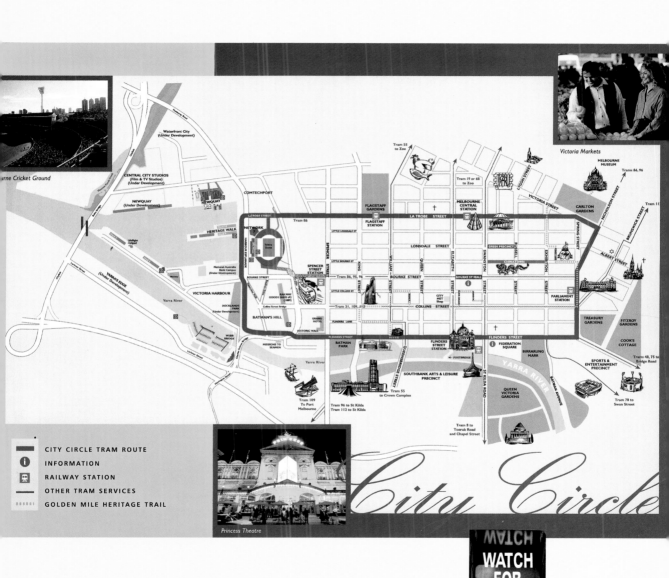

Melbourne Cricket Ground

Victoria Markets

Melbourne Museum — Trams 86, 96

Central City Studios (Film & TV Studios) (Under Development)

Newquay (Under Development)

Comtechport

Waterfront City (Under Development)

Heritage Walk

National Australia Bank Campus (Under Development)

Yarra's Edge (Under Development)

Victoria Harbour

Docklands Park (Under Development)

Webb Bridge

Batman's Hill

Yarra River

Spencer Street Station

Goods Shed #2 (BIP)

Railway Goods Shed #2 (BIP)

Collins Street Bridge

Grand Hotel

Historic Wall

Missions to Seamen

Batman Park

Tram 109 To Port Melbourne

Tram 96 to St Kilda
Tram 112 to St Kilda

Tram 55 to Crown Complex

Flinders Street Station

Footbridge

Federation Square

Birrarung Marr

Queen Victoria Gardens

Yarra River

St Kilda Road

Batman Avenue

Tram 8 to Toorak Road and Chapel Street

Southbank Arts & Leisure Precinct

Sports & Entertainment Precinct

Tram 48, 75 to Bridge Road

Tram 70 to Swan Street

Treasury Gardens

Fitzroy Gardens

Cook's Cottage

Flagstaff Gardens

Flagstaff Station

La Trobe Street

Lonsdale Street

Bourke Street

Bourke St Mall

Little Lonsdale St

Little Bourke St

Little Collins St

Flinders Lane

Collins Street

Flinders Street

City Met Shop

Melbourne Central Station

Carlton Gardens

Green Precinct

Chinatown

Parliament Station

Princess Theatre

Tram 55 to Zoo

Tram 19 or 68 to Zoo

Spencer Street

King Street

William Street

Queen Street

Elizabeth Street

Swanston Street

Russell Street

Exhibition Street

Spring Street

Albert Street

Nicholson Street

Brunswick Street

Victoria Street

Tram 112

Tram 86

Tram 86, 95, 96

Tram 31, 109, 112

Network

Telstra Dome

Legend

- CITY CIRCLE TRAM ROUTE
- INFORMATION
- RAILWAY STATION
- OTHER TRAM SERVICES
- GOLDEN MILE HERITAGE TRAIL

City Circle

WATCH FOR TRAMS

City Circle
RUNS RINGS AROUND MELBOURNE

◁ The City Circle route is operated by W series trams. Although a break with tradition, the burgundy colour scheme, with gold and cream trim and a dark green roof, clearly differentiates City Circle trams from the rest of the fleet.

▷ Caught in summer sunshine, the striking geometric shape of the Melbourne Central building has created a dominant landmark on La Trobe Street.

▽ Located opposite Parliament House is the Princess Theatre, renowned for its French Empire architecture and roll-back ventilating roof.

SAFETY ZONE

The idea of extending the city westward towards the waterfront was first raised in the late 19th century. The arrival of City Circle trams in the Docklands in 2003 introduced an unmistakable touch of Melbourne to this new and rapidly developing precinct.

The attractive timber shelter for waiting passengers at the corner of St Kilda Road and Dorcas Street, South Melbourne, is one of a number of such structures built between 1912 and 1927 in a style based on Edwardian domestic architecture. It is one of nine Melbourne tram shelters dating from this period that are listed on Victoria's Heritage Register.

△ Opened in 2002, the highly innovative shapes, colours and forms of Federation Square are a distinct contrast to the classical architecture of the buildings nearby.

▷ Students, city workers and children enjoy warm spring sunshine in Swanston Street as a colourful tram passes by.

△ Travellers have just alighted from a tram in Bourke Street at the corner of Spencer Street on a showery winter's day.

▷ The sleek shape of a European Citadis tram is dwarfed by the Gothic architecture of Australia's largest church, St Patrick's Cathedral, in Gisborne Street, East Melbourne.

▽ ▷ Completed in 1893, the tower of the Eastern Hill fire station (foreground centre) provided an observation point for the whole of the city at that time. Taller buildings in the vicinity now provide extensive views of the fire station, and tram arrivals and departures at St Vincent's Plaza nearby.

◁ ▷ The Spring Racing Carnival is renowned throughout Australia and internationally. Its premier event, the Melbourne Cup, first run in 1861, captivates the nation as horse owners, trainers, jockeys and punters eagerly await 'the first Tuesday in November'.

◁ Trams provide ready access to many European-style cafés in Melbourne's inner suburbs. The short journey along Elizabeth Street to Victoria Square enables the city's residents and visitors to enjoy the vibrant atmosphere of the Queen Victoria Market.

△ Trams on many of the routes served by Swanston Street terminate at Melbourne University to the north of the city. From there, they manoeuvre through the three-track layout to commence their journeys southward to suburbs including Toorak, Malvern and East Brighton.

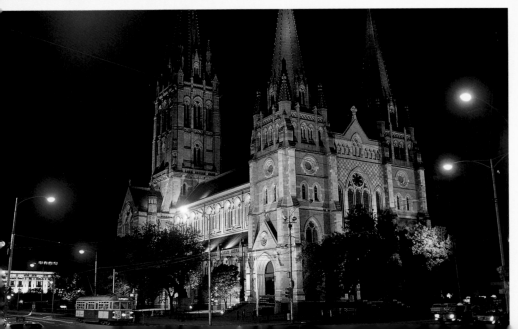

◁ Light of the world: the awe-inspiring sight of St Paul's Cathedral floodlit by night greets mid-evening tram travellers in Swanston Street.

◁ Not only is St Kilda Road one of Melbourne's finest thoroughfares; its tram lines carry more services than any other street. At least ten trams are visible in this view looking north from the Shrine.

▷ Two Z series trams in their original orange colour scheme pass at the intersection of Flinders and William streets, an area overshadowed by the viaduct completed in 1891 to connect the city's two main railway stations.

▽ Victoria Parade, East Melbourne, ranks with St Kilda Road and Royal Parade as one of the city's most attractive avenues. Amid autumn colours, a tram in the green colour scheme of the 1980s accelerates up Victoria Parade towards the city.

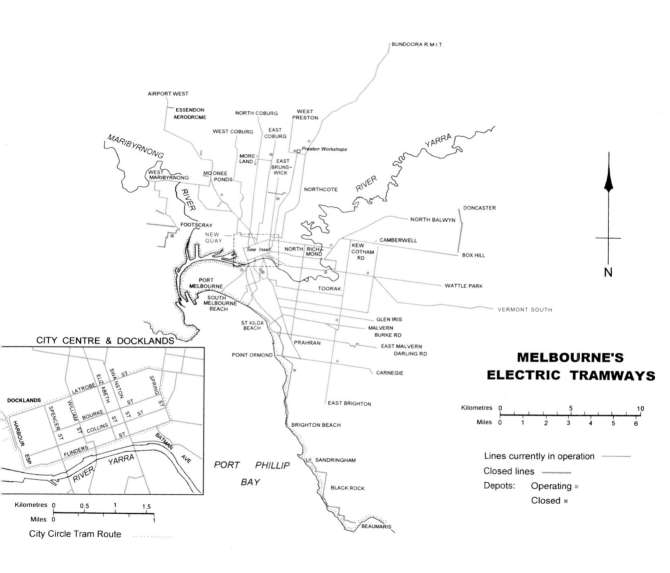

MARIBYRNONG

YARRA

RIVER

BUNDOORA R.M.I.T.

AIRPORT WEST

ESSENDON
AERODROME

NORTH COBURG

WEST
PRESTON

WEST COBURG

EAST
COBURG

Preston Workshops

MORE-
LAND

EAST
BRUNS-
WICK

WEST
MARIBYRNONG

MOONEE
PONDS

RIVER

NORTHCOTE

DONCASTER

NORTH BALWYN

FOOTSCRAY

NEW
QUAY

See Inset

NORTH
MELB.

RICH-
MOND

KEW
COTHAM
RD

CAMBERWELL

BOX HILL

PORT
MELBOURNE

TOORAK

WATTLE PARK

SOUTH
MELBOURNE
BEACH

VERMONT SOUTH

ST KILDA
BEACH

GLEN IRIS

N

MALVERN
BURKE RD

PRAHRAN

EAST MALVERN
DARLING RD

POINT ORMOND

CARNEGIE

CITY CENTRE & DOCKLANDS

EAST BRIGHTON

SWANSTON   ST

LATROBE

ELIZABETH

SPRING

DOCKLANDS

SPENCER ST

WILLIAM

BOURKE

ST

ST

ST

HARBOUR

ESP

COLLINS

ST

BATMAN

AVE

FLINDERS

YARRA

RIVER

PORT   PHILLIP
BAY

BRIGHTON BEACH

SANDRINGHAM

BLACK ROCK

| Kilometres | 0 | 0.5 | 1 | 1.5 |
| Miles | 0 | | | 1 |

City Circle Tram Route   . . . .

BEAUMARIS

MELBOURNE'S
ELECTRIC TRAMWAYS

| Kilometres | 0 | | | | | 5 | | | | | 10 |
| Miles | 0 | 1 | 2 | 3 | 4 | 5 | 6 |

Lines currently in operation ———

Closed lines ———

Depots: Operating ▪
               Closed ▪

▽ Since the mid-1980s, Port Melbourne has changed from a predominantly industrial suburb to one oriented to the residential and lifestyle needs of professional people and city workers. With the *Spirit of Tasmania II* in the background, a tram waits alongside the former Port Melbourne station.

A ride on the West Coburg tram takes passengers through Royal Park, a large expanse of land set aside in the early days of settlement. Royal Park includes an 18-hole golf course, a multitude of sporting ovals and facilities, and Melbourne's renowned Zoological Gardens. Visitors to the zoo, established in 1862 and the oldest in Australia, can return to the city by train from Royal Park station.

△ No 93 emerges from under the Royal Park railway viaduct near the rear of the Zoological Gardens, its livery blending almost perfectly with the Park's flora.

▽ Appearing more like a rural railway than a suburban tramway, the tree-lined track in Royal Park enables trams to achieve swift travelling times near the city's northern edge.

△ En route to West Maribyrnong, a tram swings from Victoria Street into Errol Street, North Melbourne.

▽ With the mist of the early morning still lingering, a near-empty tram is reflected momentarily in the calm waters of the Yarra River as it crosses Hawthorn Bridge.

▷ The undulations of Melbourne's eastern suburbs establish this vista along Riversdale Road, Camberwell, from the railway crossing in the foreground, with its distinctive boom barriers, to St Dominic's Church on the horizon.

St Kilda Junction has been a key intersection in Melbourne for well over a century, serving a host of south-eastern suburbs from St Kilda, Elwood and Brighton in the south, to Prahran, Armadale and Malvern in the east.

△ In this scene dating from around 1912, a cable tram pauses at the junction before heading north along St Kilda Road to the city.

▽ In the company of early model Holdens, trams containing homeward-bound city workers pass through St Kilda Junction on a warm summer afternoon in the mid-1950s.

▽ By the mid-1960s, acute peak-period traffic congestion at the intersection resulted in priority being given to its total reconstruction. Undertaken over several years, the work involved extensive land resumption and building demolition, numerous detours and completion of grade-separation works, which form the basis of the present arterial roads.

△ Reflected momentarily in trackside water, No 246 speeds along the tramway reservation towards Essendon Airport. Poles for overhead wiring on this part of the Essendon line were shortened and painted conspicuously because of its close proximity to the airport's east-west runway.

△ Keeping pace: articulated B series trams operate a fast and frequent service to the outer northern destination of Bundoora.

△ Eureka Skydeck 88 on Southbank offers outstanding views of the city area of Melbourne including Princes Bridge, built in 1888.

◁ A tram from Wattle Park can be glimpsed between the Federation Bells, situated in the parkland of Birrarung Marr on the north bank of the Yarra River. Combining sound with sculpture, the Federation Bells celebrate the centenary of the Commonwealth of Australia.

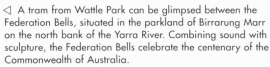

△ Leaving behind the congestion of the city, a tram heads along Macarthur Street towards the busy tramway junction at St Vincent's Plaza in East Melbourne.

◁ In breezy spring sunshine, pedestrians wait to cross Swanston Street near the Melbourne Town Hall.
.

◁ Trams have been passing the old Treasury, situated at the eastern end of Collins Street since 1886, when the Melbourne Tramway and Omnibus Company commenced running cable tram services to North Fitzroy and Victoria Bridge. Well over a century later, one of Melbourne's newest trams crosses Spring Street to reach the heart of the city.

△ Sunset on La Trobe Street Bridge.

△ Close to Box Hill terminus, a tram passes the statue of the white horse in White Horse Road.

▷ The distinctive outline of a W series tram is silhouetted against the setting sun.

▽ Collins Street at dusk.

WHAT TRAM IS THAT ?

Melbourne's tram fleet numbers some 480 vehicles, of a variety of types.

The oldest are the W series, of which approximately 50 are retained to give a heritage flavour to some services. They are loosely referred to as the 'W class', but there were originally many different varieties of Ws, classified from W through to W7, and many sub-classes. The first Ws were built in 1923. A wider body style, and improvements such as sliding doors and upholstered seats, came in the 1930s. All the Ws still in service have these refinements.

After the last W was built in 1956, a gap of almost 20 years intervened before new trams started arriving on a regular basis. These were the Z series, built between 1975 and 1984. Two hundred and thirty Zs were built, of which about 140 remain in use following deliveries of new vehicles.

Evolution in design is shown by these trams in the depot at Southbank. On the right are W series trams whose design dates from the mid-1930s, in City Circle colours and traditional green and cream; on the left is a C class tram, introduced in 2001; and in the centre is a five-unit D2 class, built in 2004.

Next came the A series, slightly shorter and with squared-off ends, compared with the tapered design of the Zs. There are 70 As, built between 1984 and 1987.

The As were followed by the B series, Melbourne's first articulated trams, with a joint above the centre wheels. The design of the vehicle body is similar to the A series. Two B1 prototypes were built in 1984 and 1985, followed by 130 B2s between 1987 and 1994, the latter introducing air conditioning to Melbourne's trams.

Privatisation of the tram system saw the introduction of new, low-floor trams imported from Europe. The ALSTOM Citadis, manufactured in France is the C class; the three-unit Siemens Combino, manufactured in Germany, is the D1 class; and the five-unit version of the Combino is the D2 class.

Drawings of the W, Z, A, B, C and D series trams appear on the following pages.

The fleet is operated from eight depots, located at Essendon, Brunswick, Preston, Kew, Camberwell, Malvern, Glen Huntly and Southbank. Maintenance is undertaken at depots; pre-delivery work on new trams and major repairs are undertaken at a large workshop in the northern suburb of Preston.

W6 class

Length	14.17 metres
Width	2.73 metres
Height	3.16 metres
Wheelbase	1575 mm truck wheelbase;
	8534 mm between truck centres
Wheel diameter	711 mm
Motors	Four 30 kW
Tare	17.7 tonnes
Seats	52
Builder	Melbourne and Metropolitan Tramways Board Workshops, Preston, Victoria

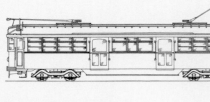

The W6 class is typical of the W series trams currently in service. These trams include the SW5, SW6, W6 and W7 classes.
The W series trams now in use were built between 1936 and 1956, and their numbers range from 728 to 1039. They run on a limited number of routes, including the City Circle service.

Z3 class

Length	16.64 metres
Width	2.67 metres
Height	3.41 metres
Wheelbase	1800 mm truck wheelbase;
	8500 mm between truck centres
Wheel diameter	660 mm
Motors	Two 195 kW
Tare	21.8 tonnes
Seats	42
Builder	Commonwealth Engineering Pty Ltd (Comeng), Dandenong, Victoria

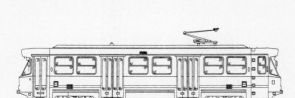

The Z series includes the Z1, Z2 and Z3 classes. Following deliveries of new C and D series trams, the Z3 class, and about 30 of the original 115 members of the earlier Z1 and Z2 classes, are in use. The drawing shows a Z3 class. The earlier Z1 and Z2 classes have two doors per side rather than three. The Z3 class also have different electrical equipment from the earlier Zs, and a new design of suspension giving improved ride quality. A new numbering system was introduced for the Z series trams, whose numbers range from 1 to 115 (Z1 and Z2 classes), and from 116 to 230 (Z3 class).

A1 and A2 classes

Numbers	231 to 300
Length	15.01 metres
Width	2.67 metres
Height	3.34 metres
Wheelbase	1800 mm truck wheelbase;
	8500 mm between truck centres
Wheel diameter	660 mm
Motors	Two 195 kW
Tare	22.2 tonnes
Seats	42
Builder	Commonwealth Engineering Pty Ltd (Comeng), Dandenong, Victoria

The body design of the A series featured improvements over the Z3 class, with rearranged doors and improved ventilation. The A2 class introduced pantographs to Melbourne's tramways, in place of the traditional trolley poles, and this means of current collection was subsequently retrofitted to the entire operational fleet. The A2 class differs from the A1 class primarily in having an improved braking system.

B1 and B2 classes

Numbers	2001 to 2132
Length	23.63 metres
Width	2.64 metres
Height	3.70 metres
Wheelbase	1800 mm truck wheelbase; 17 000 mm between outer truck centres
Wheel diameter	660 mm
Motors	Two 195 kW
Tare	34 tonnes
Seats	76
Builder	Commonwealth Engineering Pty Ltd (Comeng) and ASEA Brown Boveri (ABB), Dandenong, Victoria

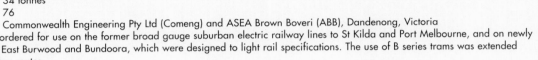

The B series were ordered for use on the former broad gauge suburban electric railway lines to St Kilda and Port Melbourne, and on newly built extensions to East Burwood and Bundoora, which were designed to light rail specifications. The use of B series trams was extended subsequently to other routes.

C class

Numbers	3001 to 3036
Length	22.69 metres
Width	2.65 metres
Height	3.27 metres
Wheelbase	1800 mm truck wheelbase; 12 840 mm between truck centres
Wheel diameter	610 mm
Motors	Four 115 kW
Tare	28.6 tonnes
Seats	40

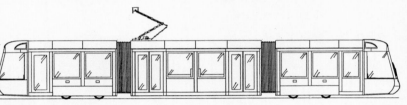

Builder and model ALSTOM, France; Citadis 300 TGA 202

The C class were the first trams to be fully imported into Australia since the mid 1920s. They incorporate many state-of-the-art features, including a full, low-floor design and video monitoring of road traffic and passenger movements on and off the vehicle.

D2 class

Numbers	5001 to 5021
Length	29.85 metres
Width	2.65 metres
Height	3.64 metres
Wheelbase	1800 mm truck wheelbase; 21 250 mm between truck centres
Wheel diameter	600 mm
Motors	Four 100 kW
Tare	35.0 tonnes
Seats	64

Builder and model Siemens Transportation, Germany; Advance Combino

The D1 class is a three-unit version of the D2 class, numbered from 3501 to 3538; both types are one hundred per cent low-floor.

△ The C and D series trams are articulated with either three or five sections, allowing these lengthy vehicles to negotiate curves with little overhang.

▽ Driver's controls on a W series tram.

▽ The control panel on a C class tram.

TRAMS IN ART

A number of distinguished artists have included trams in their paintings, either as a central theme or as incidental elements in a wider setting. Since the 1970s, trams have also become a medium to help celebrate special occasions or events. This is further recognition of the importance of trams to Melbourne and to the lives of Melburnians.

△ No 441, painted to mark Victoria's 150th anniversary in 1984, passing the former Queen Victoria Hospital in Swanston Street. This colourful tram now runs at the tramway museum in Perth.

◁ Decorated in 1990, the 'Koorie' tram promoted Victoria's Aboriginal cultural heritage.

CITY
NOLAN ST
ARTS CENTRE
DOMAIN &
ST KILDA RDS CNR
ST KILDA BEACH
CITY

▷ Stewart Merrett,
Peak Hour, 1986
Aplekage mural
Private collection

◁ Anne Graham, *Autumn in Melbourne*, 1987–88
Oil on canvas
365 cm x 122 cm
Collection of Irvin Rockman

◁ John Brack (1920–1999), *The Tram*, 1952
Oil on canvas
60 cm x 81 cm
Private collection

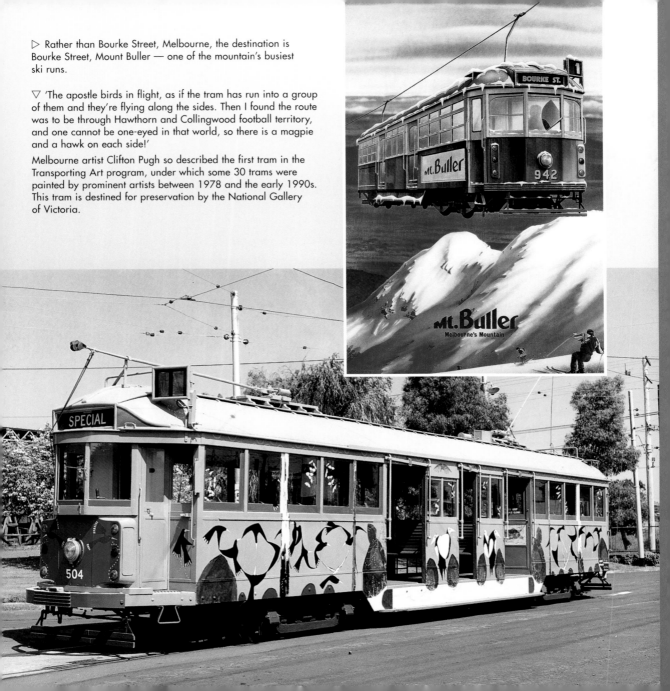

▷ Rather than Bourke Street, Melbourne, the destination is Bourke Street, Mount Buller — one of the mountain's busiest ski runs.

▽ 'The apostle birds in flight, as if the tram has run into a group of them and they're flying along the sides. Then I found the route was to be through Hawthorn and Collingwood football territory, and one cannot be one-eyed in that world, so there is a magpie and a hawk on each side!'

Melbourne artist Clifton Pugh so described the first tram in the Transporting Art program, under which some 30 trams were painted by prominent artists between 1978 and the early 1990s. This tram is destined for preservation by the National Gallery of Victoria.

BOURKE ST.

Mt.Buller

942

Mt.Buller
Melbourne's Mountain

SPECIAL

504

THE HISTORIC FLEET

Trams have been designed, built and modified over many years to meet a variety of requirements. Representatives of many of the older types now form the basis of a historic fleet that recalls how previous generations of Melburnians travelled.

◁ Although a very basic form of rail transport, horse-drawn trams offered passengers a superior ride to horse-drawn buses, which had to negotiate the rough and potholed surfaces of many 19th-century roads. A vehicle similar to this enabled Melburnians to reach the Zoo in Royal Park from the intersection of Gatehouse Street and Royal Parade between 1890 and 1923. The service came to an abrupt end following a depot fire during a police strike.

◁ No 214 was one of the largest and fastest vehicles on the road in 1906, when it entered service with the North Melbourne Electric Tramways and Lighting Company. After more than 50 years as a freight tram (see page 12) No 214 was re-converted to a 'toast-rack' passenger tram in 1978. In 2006, it was returned to the colour scheme and number, 13, which it carried a century before. The oldest electric tram in Melbourne, it is seen here in Wellington Parade, East Melbourne, with another representative vehicle of its era.

431

◁ Built in 1916 for the Hawthorn Tramways Trust, No 8 spent only 14 years in Melbourne before being sold to the State Electricity Commission for use in Bendigo. Returned to Melbourne, it was restored to near-original condition at Preston Workshops.

SCHOLARS TICKETS →

◁ Two veterans pass in La Trobe Street during a tramway cavalcade in 1979. The envy of many a museum, Birney tram No 217 represents a distinctive American design of the 1920s. Heading for East Melbourne is No 14, formerly operated by the Prahran and Malvern Tramways Trust, and visiting from Ballarat.

▷ Built in 1917 for the Melbourne, Brunswick and Coburg Tramways Trust, T class No 180 crosses the intersection of Market Street and Flinders Street.

▽ Last roll call: lined up in numerical order at South Melbourne Depot, all six members of the L class pose for a family portrait in 1975. Two of these trams, Nos 104 and 106, have been retained in the historic fleet.

△ From 1928 until withdrawals began in earnest in the 1970s, the W2 class, more than 400-strong, was synonymous with Melbourne transport. Resplendent in Hawthorn green and cream, No 510 presents the classic appearance of tram travel in the early postwar years.

△ Magnificently restored to the original 1923 W class design, distinguished by three equal-width doorways, No 380 poses for its portrait in Simpson Street, East Melbourne.

▽ Passengers on W1 class trams, introduced in 1925, were able to enjoy open-air seating reminiscent of cable grip cars, then being replaced by electric trams. Popular in warm weather but less satisfactory in winter, the open centre sections were enclosed within little more than a decade.

△◁ Nos 469 and 613 were among a small group of experimental trams built in 1927 and 1930 that reflected design trends in North America. These trams owe their longevity to their suitability for training drivers because of the unobstructed access to the driver's position.

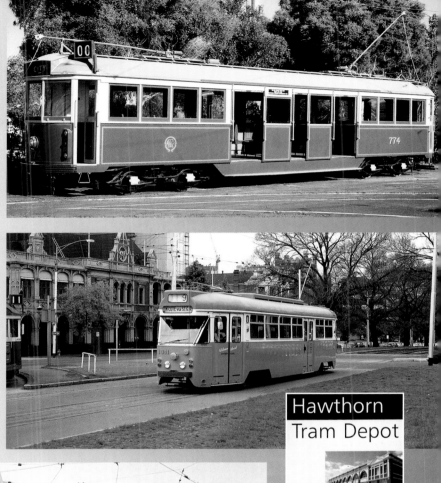

△ Melbourne's last single-truck trams were built in 1930 to improve service standards on short-distance lines such as Point Ormond and the Footscray system. No 676 presents an image of modernity as it passes a slow-moving 'Ransome' steam wagon in Wellington Parade.

▷ Improvements in passenger safety and comfort, and replacement of worn-out parts, often led to the alteration or removal of distinctive original features. No 774, one of 120 W5 class trams built between 1935 and 1939, was the only one of its class to survive with its original three-door, drop-centre section and square-cornered windshields. It was returned to its prewar colour scheme in 1993.

▷ Built as the prototype for a proposed new fleet of modern trams, No 1041 entered service in 1973. It demonstrated many design features that were adopted in the later Z series trams.

▽ Closed to routine operations in 1965, Hawthorn Depot now houses the historic tram fleet. Some of the depot's occupants are seen on display in 1992.

Hawthorn Tram Depot

CHANGING
COLOURS

The trams pictured in this book show a variety of colour schemes, reflecting the multiplicity of liveries that have been applied, particularly in recent years.

For almost 50 years from 1925, Melbourne's trams were painted green and cream, common colours for trams in many cities. The introduction of a completely new design of tram in 1973 was accompanied by a new colour scheme, predominantly orange. Since then there has been a succession of variations and changes as the pictures in this section show.

Restructuring of Victoria's public transport organisations in 1983 brought a reversion to colours which were closer to the earlier green and cream. The shades chosen were similar to Australia's national colours of green and gold. Starting in 2000, all but the W series began to be painted in completely different colours following privatisation. Each of the two initial operators adopted a distinctive colour scheme as shown in these pages. Currently the sole operating company, Yarra Trams, has corporate colours of white (formerly light grey) with trim colours of green and blue.

In addition to these comings and goings, the collective appearance of the trams is varied by those painted for advertising purposes or for special events, while the restaurant trams carry their own distinctive livery.

◁ In 1994, ten W series trams were painted in a distinctive colour scheme for the City Circle service. In a further initiative that year, W series trams selected for retention reverted to their original green and cream colours complete with gold lining, a refinement that had been dropped in the 1960s. Nos 1027 and 925 display these contrasting liveries.

△ The first of the Z series trams, introduced in 1975, were painted orange. From 1979, a variation of the Z series design was accompanied by a modified colour scheme of deep yellow. The orange and yellow colours were never applied to W series trams, which continued to be painted in the traditional green and cream.

▽ The last of the B2 trams is seen fresh from the factory in 1994.

The Met 961

◁ The long-lived green and cream colours of the Melbourne and Metropolitan Tramways Board are seen to advantage in this view of two brand-new W series trams — among the last of their type to be built — in Glenferrie Road on the railway crossing at Kooyong in January 1956.

△ The shock of the new: the orange livery introduced by the Z series trams was a bright contrast to the traditional colours of the past. No 10 was only a few weeks old when this picture was taken in 1975. The tram at far left, used for track cleaning, shows a colour scheme reserved for non-passenger trams.

◁ From 1983 Melbourne's trams, including these at Kew Depot, were painted in colours whose official names were Shamrock Green and Wattle Yellow, intended to represent Australia's national colours of green and gold.

DRIVERS UNTIE ROPES & RELEASE FROM CLIPS

▷ Two brand-new Z series trams show off their orange colour scheme in 1975.

BEWARE OF TRAM DEPOT

▷ Privatisation of Melbourne's trams in August 1999 initially brought two new operating companies and two new liveries. Within five years Yarra trams became responsible for the entire system. Their colours are shown in this picture taken on the occasion of the launch of their new Citadis trams in October 2001. W series trams have not been painted in new colours: they remain in the two colour schemes shown on page 44.

◁ The bright M>Tram colour scheme is shown to good effect by this brand-new Combino tram in St Kilda Road. The withdrawal of M>Tram's parent company from its operating franchise resulted in this livery being short-lived.

◁ Adoption of light grey as a basic colour, with stylised application of blue and green, provided a fresh appearance for trams such as No 2077, pictured in Bourke Street. The current Yarra Trams livery uses white as its base colour, and the trim has been varied from that carried by the tram in this picture.

▽ Trams can run through only shallow water before risking damage to their electrical equipment. But drivers brave enough to speed through water can create quite a bow wave, as shown by this photo taken in Nicholson Street, Carlton.

△ A torrential downpour in February 1972 halted tram services in the area now occupied by the Bourke Street Mall. The situation soon deteriorated into a flash flood, with the trams marooned and a panel van well afloat.

OUT OF THE ORDINARY

The primary role of trams is to provide reliable services for commuters and other travellers. They can also perform other roles, including providing special services in response to popular demand and participating in festivities. And unexpected weather can test the best-prepared organisation.

For several years Trams on Parade was the centrepiece of Melbourne's autumn Moomba procession along St Kilda Road and Swanston Street. As these scenes show, trams decorated in gaudy colours or transformed into zany designs attracted large crowds. Trams from other cities, near and far, also captured the interest of the locals.

◁ Half a world away from its home city, this 70-year-old veteran from Milan provides a memorable outing for members of Melbourne's Italian community as it journeys around the City Circle.

△ Right of way would be assured by this colourful design.

◁ A long way from sand and surf, a 'Bondi Tram' from Sydney crosses Princes Bridge.

△ The centenary of Melbourne's electric trams in 2006 saw a colourful display of trams old and new at Docklands.

▷ Complete with boxes and bundles on its roof, this tram has been intricately decorated to represent travel in Asia.

Melbourne's streets are filled with restaurants.

At a slumbering 20 kph on a super absorbent suspension system, it's hardly fast food. But even at this pace, a 5 star meal on the only mobile tramcar restaurant in the world will go by too quickly. And with good reason. As soon as you enter this 1927 vintage world class tram, with its luxurious Pullman style decor and mouth watering dishes of all Victorian produce, you'll wish it never stopped. You can catch it for a 3 to 5 course lunch or dinner. Even the view has several courses to choose from—Toorak Road, Fitzroy Street, Acland Street. Victoria Street and Southgate — are just a few of the directions you can go. And these destinations are not just for the Restaurant tram. They're just some of the fabulous culinary routes you can travel down for a memorable dining experience in Melbourne. There's everything from Japanese to Zulu, from Malaysian to Hungarian. If you love great food and haven't experienced Melbourne's restaurant circuit ask for a menu. Call Tourism Victoria on 1800 63 77 63 for your free copy of The Melbourne Brochure.

◁ ▽ Restaurant trams have become a distinctive feature of the city. Since the venture began in 1984, the restaurant fleet has grown to three vehicles, each with seating for 36 patrons. Excellent food is complemented by the high-quality decor of these trams, which are popular with individuals and groups alike.

▷ The film *Malcolm* centred on the exploits of a tram buff whose ability with gadgets led to a successful criminal career. In this scene, filmed at the former depot at South Melbourne, Colin Friels in the title role is setting off with his homemade tram for an early morning run.

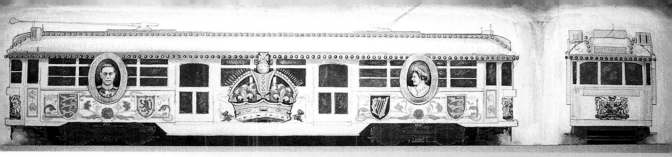

△ The death of
King George VI in 1952
caused the cancellation
of a planned royal tour of
Australia, and as a result
this design for an attractively
decorated tram never saw
the light of day.

▽ John Hargreaves, Colin
Friels and Lindy Davies pose
with the later version of
Malcolm's unusual getaway
tram. *Malcolm* was directed
by Nadia Tass and released
by Cascade Films in 1986.

▽ In 1962 the Melbourne
and Metropolitan Tramways
Board proposed a scheme
for trams in the central
city area to be placed
underground. Tunnels were
to run beneath Swanston and
Bourke Street, but prohibitive
costs led to the plan being
abandoned.

CARE AND MAINTENANCE

Like other major undertakings, Melbourne's tramways require facilities and staff committed to carrying out maintenance and improvements.

NOT IN SERVICE

◁ Evening at Malvern Depot.

△ Trams undergo inspection at Preston Workshops.

△ Spared the hazards of weekday congestion, track workers repair a section of track in Collins Street on a quiet Sunday morning.

◁ Despite the advent of innovations such as dot-matrix indicators, some trams retain fabric destination rolls. What appears to be white lettering on a black background is actually produced by applying black paint to a white surface to produce the required combination of suburbs and street names. Here, a painter at Preston Workshops prepares new rolls for use in W series trams.

THEN & NOW

Growth and redevelopment of cities and suburbs can result in constant change to streetscapes and landmarks, or the demise of once-familiar modes of transport. Steady transformation seems to be particularly apparent in the central business districts of Melbourne and other large cities. However, in some other places little seems to have changed in more than half a century.

◁ End of the working week: With the clocks on Flinders Street Station showing 12.20 pm on a Saturday, pedestrians, trams and horse-drawn wagons compete for road space. When this picture was taken in 1927, electric trams had taken over in Swanston Street but the cable trams on the Richmond line still ran in Flinders Street.

△ The scene from the same vantage point 68 years later in 1995. Two of the three structures visible, Flinders Street Station (centre) and Young and Jackson's Hotel (right), remain as familiar landmarks for future generations. Although this photograph was taken during the morning peak hour, the advent of the underground rail loop has made this area less of a focal point for commuters.

In the early 1970s, some years before their conversion to light rail, the St Kilda and Port Melbourne railway lines were the domain of the Victorian Railways' most antiquated carriages. At right, a swing-door electric train crosses Albert Road, South Melbourne, shortly before the withdrawal of this type of rollingstock in 1974; above, two of Melbourne's most modern trams are seen at the same location in 2004.

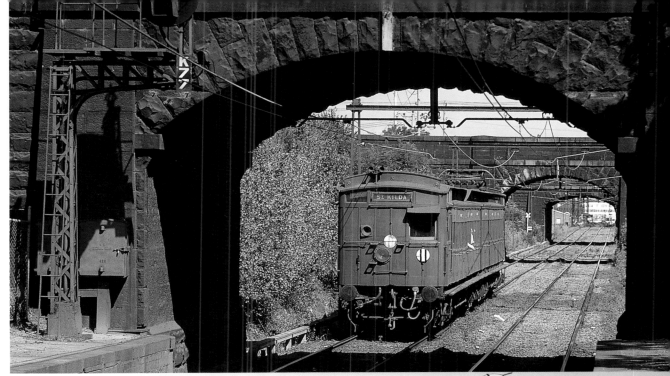

CUT OFF

Apart from peak periods, patronage on the St Kilda line rarely required trains of more than two carriages. One such train, and its successor, a D series tram, are seen leaving South Melbourne. Trams replaced trains on this line in 1987.

A distinguishing feature of Melbourne's tram system is that relatively little track has been closed. An example of a rare closure is the last few hundred metres of the former line to Essendon Aerodrome, shown in 1969, which was alongside Vaughan Street. Closed in 1976 when the route was diverted to Airport West, almost no evidence remains today of the track leading to the former terminus.

Trams first crossed the Maribyrnong River in 1940 to serve the Explosives Factory at West Maribyrnong. Built originally as a single-track bridge, the tramway viaduct was duplicated in 1943, in line with the growth in wartime traffic on the West Maribyrnong line. For the next 27 years, an unusual feature of the river crossing was the existence of separate road and tramway bridges. A new bridge for both motor vehicles and trams was completed in 1967.

▷ Petrol rationing and crew shortages stretched tram services to the limit during the Second World War. With passengers clinging to every foothold, No 244 edges its way along Brunswick Street towards the Fitzroy football ground in 1944.

▷ The scene today: Fitzroy Football Club has moved to Brisbane, and commuters passing the same location face a far less challenging journey home. And No 244? It now operates a tourist service in Christchurch, New Zealand.

△ Unpopular with business and community leaders for decades, the extensive railway sidings and workshops between the city and the Yarra River were progressively removed from the mid-1980s.

▷ Opened in 1999, the Batman Avenue bridge provides access to Melbourne Park and other major sporting and entertainment facilities to the east of the city. Only just visible in this high-angle view, a tram returning from Wattle Park crosses the bridge en route to Flinders Street.

△ The use of trams for advertising began early, with a tram used to promote recruitment during the First World War, as shown on page 12. In the 1940s, trams were occasionally used for special campaigns, which tended to be community-based rather than commercially oriented, such as this savings campaign in 1945.

MOBILE BILLBOARDS

Plentiful in number and travelling extensively throughout the city and suburbs, trams and other forms of public transport provide a convenient way of advertising products and promoting community causes.

◁ The 'Parade of Homes' exhibition in the mid-1950s was promoted by this large sign on a tram that doubled as a freight tram carrying stores from Preston Workshops to the various tram depots throughout Melbourne.

△ Well-chosen words promote the musical *Les Miserables*.

△ This articulated tram was brightly painted for a proposed housing development at Port Melbourne, marketed under its original name of Sandridge.

▽ Chinese red provides a great visual impact on the tram painted in 1988 to promote both Melbourne's sister city relationship with Jiangsu, and the associated visit of pandas to the Melbourne Zoo.

▽ 'Slip, slop, slap on sunscreen' is No 293's bold message to sun seekers.

△ ▷ These trams entice people to visit the Melbourne Zoo or to join the Royal Australian Navy.

Techniques developed in recent years enable an advertisement to extend across a tram's windows.

▽ Catch *The Wizard of Oz* tram to the Regent Theatre in Collins Street.

Trams are so well etched in the minds of Melburnians that they not only display advertising but become part of the message, as shown by these three examples.

GONE BUT NOT FORGOTTEN

Tram networks are dynamic. Like other transport systems, they may grow or contract, and lines may be relocated from time to time to meet changing community needs.

The story of Melbourne's electric tram network is a positive one. Except for the 1960s, the network grew in every decade of the 20th century, and this trend is likely to continue. For those who appreciate and enjoy the benefits of tram travel it is fortunate that the few closures that occurred in the postwar years did not mark the beginning of a general contraction of the system.

Operated as a separate entity from 1921, the Footscray lines were isolated from the main tramway system until connecting track was laid in Maidstone in 1954. The combination of small, four-wheel trams and three short lines gave the system a quaintness that resembled the tramways of Ballarat, Bendigo or Geelong rather than those elsewhere in Melbourne. The Footscray local network closed in 1962.

△ Built by the Victorian Railways' Newport Workshops in 1923, No 41 was restored to its striking original livery in Bendigo in 2005.

In Melbourne's bayside suburbs, the Victorian Railways operated two 'electric street railways'. The first of these, which opened in two stages in 1906, was a broad gauge line (1600 mm gauge, the same as the suburban railways) between St Kilda railway station and Brighton Beach railway station. This line was the first successful electric tramway in Melbourne, following the short-lived Box Hill to Doncaster line, which operated from 1889 to 1896. The second Victorian Railways line, which opened in 1919, was of standard gauge and ran between Sandringham and Black Rock. From 1926 to 1931 this line extended a further 3.5 kilometres to Beaumaris.

As a minor adjunct to the State's rail services, the 'railway trams' never enjoyed the attention given to their counterparts elsewhere in Melbourne. Low investment and sporadic interest by railway administrators led to the closure of the Sandringham–Black Rock line in 1956, followed by the demise of the St Kilda–Brighton Beach line in 1959.

A shuttle service operated along Glen Huntly Road between Point Ormond and Elsternwick railway station until October 1960, when it was replaced by a bus service.

△ With passengers from the connecting bus on board, No 48 is shown in 1954 before its departure from Black Rock for Sandringham, 4 kilometres to the north.

▽ If the early 20th-century residents of Melbourne's inner south-eastern suburbs had had their way, the St Kilda to Brighton Beach tramway would have been a railway. In the event this was not to be, and for over 50 years St Kilda station served as an interchange point between suburban trains and the feeder tramway.

▽ Different appearance, different gauges, different management. Victorian Railways tram No 43 meets No 894 of the Melbourne and Metropolitan Tramways Board as it crosses the standard gauge track in Fitzroy Street to reach St Kilda railway station.

◁ As summer twilight turns to evening, a tram waits for passengers at St Kilda station during the final weeks of the Brighton Beach line in 1959.

△ Trams on two lines now closed: Victorian Railways No 43 waits in Broadway, Elwood, while No 677 of the Melbourne and Metropolitan Tramways Board heads east along Glen Huntly Road from Point Ormond.

▽ On a clear autumn day in 1957, a tram waits for passengers at Point Ormond terminus, set in parkland near Point Ormond Road.

POINT ORMOND
ELSTERNWICK RLY STN
SOUTH CAULFIELD JUN
GLENHTLY DEPOT
SPECIAL

▷ Bound for Ballarat Road, No 465 swings from Hopkins Street, Footscray, into Droop Street in the early 1950s.

▽ Apart from their size, Footscray trams could be readily distinguished from others in Melbourne by their destination signs, which included 'Pyrotechnic Factory', 'Explosives Factory' and other intriguing locations.

EXPLOSIVES FTY
ORDNANCE FTY
DEPOT
WILLIAMSTOWN RD
RAILWAY STATION
RUSSELL ST
BALLARAT RD
SPECIAL
FOOTBALL GROUND
AMMUNITION FTY
PYROTECHNIC FTY
CITY VIA HAYMARKET
SPECIAL . E

▷ Unfazed by local traffic, a tram driver goes about his task of picking up and setting down passengers in Barkly Street, en route to Russell Street, West Footscray.

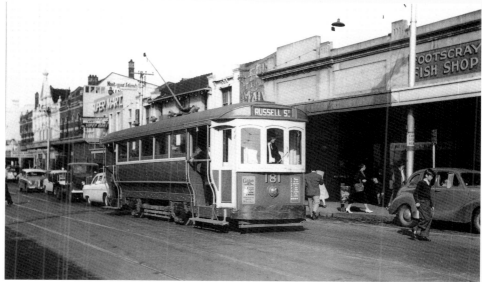

△ A city-bound tram makes its way along the former Batman Avenue on the north bank of the Yarra River. In 1999, this section of line was re-routed to reach Flinders Street at Exhibition Street.

▷ A scene from the past: football crowds wait eagerly for their city-bound trams, while others with time to spare stroll westward along Wellington Parade towards Flinders Street.

IN GREENER PASTURES

What happens to Melbourne's trams when they finish their useful lives?

The answer used to be, in many cases, that they went on to new careers in Victoria's major provincial cities. Geelong, Ballarat and Bendigo all had tram systems, operated by the State Electricity Commission. Virtually all of the trams used on these networks were second-hand vehicles from Melbourne.

Trams in these three cities were all replaced by buses. In Geelong the last service finished in 1956, with final closures occurring in Ballarat in 1971 and in Bendigo in 1972. However, in both Ballarat and Bendigo, parts of the tram systems have been retained for museum or tourist operations.

Of course, not all of Melbourne's retired trams went to the three major provincial cities. Many were stripped of wheels, motors and other electrical equipment, and sold for use as sheds, while others were simply scrapped.

In the 1970s, the advent of the Z series trams led to the disposal of large numbers of early W series trams. Although old, they were serviceable, and a market developed for their sale in complete condition, ready for further operation.

Many W series trams were made available to museums in Australia and overseas, while others were sold for use on tram systems in the United States. Today, trams from Melbourne are in daily service in locations as diverse as San Francisco, Seattle and Memphis. One is in England, bought by Elton John for his garden. Since 1990, retired W series trams have been retained in storage; in recent years withdrawn Zs have been sold, with some being donated to museums.

Melbourne has its own tram museum, operated by the Tramway Museum Society of Victoria at Bylands, near Kilmore, 65 kilometres north of Melbourne. A number of historic trams are retained in Melbourne itself, and are depicted in 'The Historic Fleet' (pp. 39–43).

▷ Far from the Melbourne suburbs where it began its career, a tram passes through Ironbark Gully on its way from Bendigo to the outlying suburb of Eaglehawk.

▷ Restored to its original appearance, No 44 of the Prahran and Malvern Tramways Trust is seen in a Bendigo setting reminiscent of suburban Melbourne about the time of the First World War.

▷ The Shamrock Hotel provides a handsome background for a tram in Pall Mall, Bendigo. Built in 1914 for the Prahran and Malvern Tramways Trust, it was bought by the State Electricity Commission for use in Bendigo in 1951. A tourist service operated by the Bendigo Trust now runs on this section of track.

△ The tradition of retired Melbourne trams having new leases of life in the provincial cities has continued, with the tourist and museum lines in Bendigo and Ballarat both receiving W series trams from Melbourne in recent years. Here, one such tram is seen from the verandah of the Shamrock Hotel.

◁ Beautifully restored by the Ballarat Tramway Preservation Society, No 26 poses for its portrait on the section of Ballarat's tramways now operated as a museum line. This is how No 26 looked when it entered service in Ballarat in 1930, little different from its original appearance when built for the Hawthorn Tramways Trust in 1916.

◁ Ballarat is typical of the cities that were too small to sustain tram systems. Two trams are seen en route from Mount Pleasant shortly before the end of operations in 1971. Happily, a short section of track alongside Lake Wendouree is still used for a heritage tramway.

▷ The Tramway Museum Society of Victoria's trams run on a section of former railway line through open countryside near Bylands. A W1 class tram gives its passengers a breezy ride as it rolls along the Museum's track.

▷ The city of Christchurch, New Zealand, opened a new tourist tramway in 1995. Trams run on a circular route around the city centre, and the service has been so popular that two ex-Melbourne trams have been imported to provide extra capacity. No 411 is a handsome sight in its new guise as a restaurant tram.

△ Around 25 trams of the W series, withdrawn from the 1970s onwards, were exported to the United States, where many now run on mainly tourist-oriented services. Memphis has 11 former Melbourne trams, the largest such fleet, and they are painted in a variety of bright colours. This example is pictured beside the Mississippi River.

△ Luna Park, the home of this
retired tram, provides a fun
venue for children's birthday
parties.

Luna party tram

PICTURE SOURCES

All photographs by authors except the following